Dr. Steve Vandegriff

Campus Ministry

Academx
Publishing Services

Permissions Department
Academx Publishing Services, Inc.
P.O. Box 208
Sagamore Beach, MA 02562

Printed in the United States of America

ISBN-10. 1-60036-567-1
ISBN-13: 978-1-60036-567-6

TABLE OF CONTENTS

CULTURE

Major Influences Shaping Our Culture

I.   Introduction
A. _____ asks an important question, "When the foundations are being destroyed, _____ _____ _____ _____ ____?"

B. Definition of missionary _____
_____.

C. _____ _____ has become that mission field.

II. Six Influences Shaping Our Culture
A. _____ ____ _____ _____

"There is one thing a professor can be absolutely certain of: almost every student entering the university believes or says he believes…that truth is relative." *Allan Bloom* in Closing of the American Mind.

1.   Good is what one finds _____.

2.   There are two restrictions:
   a. _____.
   b. _____ (defies nature; the line is _____ between man and the rest of creation; Gen. 9:3-6) _____).

3. Values are collected from:
   a.
   b.
   c.
   d.
   e.

Values We Can Agree On
1.
2.
3.
4.
5.
6.
7.
8.
9.
10.
11.
12.
13.
14.
15.
16.
17.
18.
19.
20.

Values We Disagree On

1.
2.
3.
4.
5.
6.
7.
8.

B. _____ _____
    1. Deterioration of _____ _____
    2. Domination of _____ _____ _____
    3. Dealing with the _____ _____/_____ _____
    4. Do you have it better than your parents?
C. _____ has become our most important commodity.
    1. _____-has not delivered the leisure it advertises; on the contrary, _____ _____ _____ _____; we fill the time we've gained with more work.

Tech Revolt

1. The Problem
    Technology _____
    _____ of the _____
    Teeth-gnashing demands of _____ _____
    at work/home
    Obsession over _____-_____ _____
    Addiction to _____ _____
    Onslaught of _____
    Mind numbing complexity of
    _____/_____
    Dot.com _____

2. The Good Side
    High tech advances have _____ ____
    _____
    Sped up _____
    _____ our lives

3. Dark Side
    _____ our lives
    _____ us to our _____
    _____ our _____

"Technology was supposed to free us and make our lives easier, but it has done the opposite. IT is creating havoc in our lives. Everyone is overwhelmed and stressed out." Psychologist Francine Toder, Palo Alto, California

"We have to live in balance with all this technology. If we're always hurrying to have the latest computer or the best new job, we're going to miss our lives. We need to ask ourselves: What is really important?"
Cecile Andrews, Stanford University visiting scholar

2. _____ _____ contribute to the _____
   _____. (It takes ____ _____ ____ _____ to fund the
   lifestyles we have chosen.)
3. Traded _____ for _____…leaving no time to relax or parent
   our students.

D. Pursuit of _____-_____

1. Wanda Urbanska in <u>The Singular Generation</u>, writes:
   -we have nothing to _____ _____ _____
   -we have never learned _____ _____ _____ (in _____, in _____,
   in _____, in _____ and _____ _____)
   -instead, we have narrowed our scope of vision to the small picture:
   _____ _____ _____, _____ _____, _____ _____

2. This generation has been let down over and over again
   -
   -
   -
   -
   -

3. The Price? _____ ____ _____ ____ _____
   _____ _____, whether in marriage, families,
   or friends

E. Redefining ____ ____ _____
   1. _____ _____ _____
   2. _____ ____ ____ _____
   3. _____ vs. _____
   4. _____ _____ _____ to influence the values of their
      students

F. Increase in Personal and Social Destructive Behavior

III. Why are God's People Here?

    A. Psalms 11:3, "_____ ____ ____ _____ ___?"

    B. _____, "and gave us the ministry of reconciliation."

    C. Definition of reconcile: _____

    _____.

    D. Ambassador Characteristics (II Corinthians 5:20)
        1. An ambassador is a representative of his own culture
        2. An ambassador is sensitive to the host culture
        3. An ambassador informs the host country of his countries policies, even to
        the point of protests.
        4. An ambassador is called back to his country when his term is up or if it is
        too dangerous.

    E. All of life can be ministry!

Incarnational Witness

I. The Life and Ministry of Christ
    A. John 1:1-5,14- _____ _____ __ _____
        1. ____ _____-God took the first step by _____ __ ____
          Application:
                Open-minded to what public school says
                Reach them where they are
                Pro-active instead of reactive
                Understood and knew how to relate
                Overlook outward appearance
                Students are more than a soul
                Sacrifice

        2. ____ _____-God permeated the world with ____ _____ ___ _____ _____
          Application:
                Walk the walk
                May not be welcomed
                Well thought out plan
                No compromise/no retreat
                Service
                Prepared
                Willing to go into foreign territory

        3. ____ _____-God identified with _____ _____ _____.
          a. Application
                Addressed physical/spiritual needs
                Take time to understand
                Finding common ground
                Remember your adolescence

          b. Adolescent's deepest needs
                Accountability
                Meaningful Relationships
                Attention
                Time

Name
Consistency
Affection
Acceptance/Love
Stability
Role Model

B. We are empowered to _____ _____ _____ _____
_____ (Are we comfortable among unchurched students?).

C. We can _____ ____ _____ _____ for who they are.

D. We can _____ _____ _____ ___ _____ to them.

II. How Can We Incarnate Ourselves in the Adolescent World?

   A. _____ and _____
       1. We cannot wait for students to come to us, but rather ____ _____
       ____ ____ ____ _____.

       2. This means moving from what is _____ ____ _____
       ___ _____.
       3. It means crossing barriers of _____, _____, and ____.

   B. Identification
       1. We need to "_____ _____ _____" and learn ____ _____
       _____ _____ _____ ("Hanging out with purpose")
       2. We need to learn how to _____ _____ _____ with them.
       3. This is very _____ and _____ _____.

The Psychology of Unregenerated Young People

1. They have rejected the _____, but that doesn't necessarily mean that he has _____ _____.
    a. Church is seen as _____ and _____
    b. Many non-Christians believe that the church isn't very_____
    ____ _____ _____

2. They are _____ _____, but secretly want an "_____"
    a. Americans still believe in all _____ _____
    b. Many hold the attitude that there are no _____ _____
    _____ but ethics should _____ _____ ___
    _____ _____ (usually a person's own selfish agenda)
    c. many are seeking _____ _____ for their lives

3. They resist _____ but respond to _____.
    a. doesn't like to be _____ _____ ___ ___
    b. not convinced the Bible is _____ _____ _____
    c. has been a society-wide erosion of _____ ___ _____
    d. open to _____
    e. need to lay out the underlying thinking behind _____ _____
    _____
    f. needs to know the _____ of _____ by God's _____

4. They do not understand _____, but is also ignorant about what ____ _____ ___ _____ ___.
    a. _____ _____
        -most people can't name the four Gospels
        -many do not know who delivered the Sermon on the Mt.
        -many do not know why Christians celebrate Easter
    b. doesn't have a handle on _____ _____ _____
    c. effective evangelism approach:
        -

        -

        -

        -

5. They have _____ _____ about _____ matters, but doesn't expect _____ _____ _____.

    a. many look at churches and 'see' a sign..._____ _____ _____

    b. Hebrews 11:6, "rewards those who earnestly seek Him."

    c. the manner in which we _____, determines if he'll go deeper about _____ ____ ____ _____ _____

6. They don't just ask, "___ _____ _____?" but "_____ _____ _____?"

    a. the God of the Bible offers us _____/_____ in our struggles, difficulties and _____ from past hurts

    b. the reason it works _____ ____ ____ _____

7. They do not just want to _____ _____; they want to experience it. The objective of evangelism is to _____ _____ in to an _____ _____ _____, not just pass information about God.

8. They do not want to be _____ _____, but would like to be _____ _____.

    a. have you ever had a friendship with _____ _____?

    b. unchurched feel that the main reason for friendship is because we want ____ _____ _____

    c. real friendship is based upon:

        -

        -

        -

        -

    d. unchurched guys are more desperate for _____ _____ and less equipped to find them

    e. David W. Smith's, <u>Men Without Friends</u> suggest why:

        -as youngsters, we're _____ to _____ _____

        -___ _____

        -keep _____ _____ and _____ _____ _____

        -have role models that are _____ and _____

9. They may trust authority, but is receptive to _____ _____ _____

a. turned off by:

-
-
-
-
-

b. they respond to:

-
-
-
-
-

10. They are no longer _____ to _____, but is attracted to places where his needs will be met.

11. They are not much of a _____, but are hungry for a _____ ____ _____ _____ _____.

12. Even though they may not be _____ _____, they want to get quality _____ _____.

13. They are confused about ____ _____, but they don't know that the _____ ____ _____ for them what it means to be a ____ or _____.

14. They are proud that they are _____ of different _____, but think that Christians are _____-_____.
    a.
    b.

15. There's a good chance they would try church if a _____ _____ _____, but this may actually do more _____ _____ _____
    a. what will _____ _____ _____?
    b. remember that many stopped or don't go for a reason

    -
    -
    -
    -
    -

    c. danger is that they may go and find that nothing has changed or it was just as they expected

Trends

I.   Introduction
         A. A world of Excess
         B. A world of Access
         C. There is choice to the nth degree

II. Trends
         A. Definition-a label that often identifies a movement
         Trends affect our lifestyle
         Trends affect our purchasing decisions
         Trends eventually give us a new outlook

         B.   The tracking of so-called 'trends' and 'what's cool' is a hot topic these days,
         mainly because mainstream businesses have been trying to crack the tastes,
         preferences and styles of the elusive and fickle youth culture. With over $172
         billion of expendable income, everybody wants a piece of these 'cool' spenders.

         C.   We are anxiously awaiting a rebellious and radical surge from this youth
         culture.
         BUT WHY WAIT? Look around and listen.

III. Virtual Faith[1]

         A.   Religious statements about this generation must take pop (popular) culture
         into account.

         B.   Being a latchkey kid, raised in loco parentis, television and the Internet
         provides daily entertainment. This generation spends more time with technology
         than with parents, during childhood.

         C.   Video games encourage technological literacy blurring the distinction between
         work and play.

         D.   There is a tolerance of religious diversity.

         E.   This generation is not only personally learned about the fragility of
         commitment but has also been forced into a premature and untutored adulthood.

         F.   Previous generations had the Vietnam War, WWII, the Great Depression, and
         WWI as rallying points. This generation has never wept in public for the memory
         of a great leader or a great movement, until 9.11.

---

[1] Beaudoin, Tom. Virtual Faith: The Irreverent Spiritual Quest of Generation X. San Francisco: Jossey-Bass, 1998.

G.   Prior to 9.11, in 1989, two epic events: Tiananmen Square massacre and the Fall of the Berlin Wall. Churches seemed laughingly out of touch; they had hopelessly droll music antediluvian technology, retrograde social teaching, and hostile or indifferent attitudes toward popular culture.

H.   There are plenty of reasons for this current generation to feel anxious. This generation bears the weight of so many failures-including AIDS, divorce, abuse, poor schools, recessions, youth poverty, teen suicide, outrageous educational and living expenses, failure of religious institutions, national debt, high taxes, environmental devastation, drugs, parents that need to be parented, violence, unstable economic security, premature loss of childhood.

I.   Churches can have a welcome opportunity to give meaning and significance to a student's life.

J.   This youth culture is the most resourceful, intellectual, and creative generation that we have seen in the past fifty years.

K.   This generation is a force seeking out their own partnerships, mentors, avenues of capital spending, and platforms for communicating.

IV.   Distinctives

A. Youth today are all one big sample of _____. Through the media, technology and society, we've all been exposed to other _____ and

_____.

B. Diversity has taught us to celebrate our _____ and to enjoy the _____ of others.

C. Today's youth culture is the most _____ _____ to date.

D. Society is moving rapidly to a ____-_____ _____ population.

E. There will be an integration of _____, _____ _____,

_____, and _____.

F. This culture is no longer programmed to believe in _____ _____ or become reliant on _____ _____.

G. So why do mainstream youth today pierce other parts besides the ear? The body is the one thing they can own and alter.

H. Freestyle sports, a.k.a. "_____" sports, are another example of what the streets have been doing and how they have infiltrated the mainstream.

I. *Extreme* sports earned their label because the athletes who participate in these sports play _____ the _____ of _____

_____ _____.

J. The____-____ culture is a lifestyle with its own language, style of dress, music
and mind-set. (Rap emerged from Hip-Hop).

K. *Freestyle* is the morphing of _____, _____, and _____.

Freestyle is a _____ _____ _____. This doesn't mean chaos and anarchy. It is a mindset that is _____ and _____ by _____.

Freestyle is about everything this generation believes in:

-

-

-

(An example of freestyle culture is skateboarding.)

VI.   Conclusion:

A. Their sense of graphics and color are different.
It is not enough to create a symbol. They will be those of the emotions and ideologies of the street cultures. Be _____, look _____, not _____.

B. There is a fusion happening on the streets. Diverse cultures are borrowing and mixing influences from one another. It is happening in music, fashion, and in venues where they congregate.

C. The solution is for us to edit and sift through the excitement and energy of what this young person is saying AND get to the content. There is always a unifying theme, a consistent point of view that spreads throughout youth cultures.

The Millennials

Introduction
-We cannot be too _____ or _____ about this generation
-Each extreme result in _____
-We must be _____

M's have known only _____ and _____.
They have been lulled into _____.
They are the most _____ _____ _____ in history. (Marketers
know what's going into students' lives, and they know what is not going into students' lives. DO
YOU?)

Their World
1. A new way of looking at life.
A world-view is a set of presuppositions (assumptions which may be true,
partially true or entirely false) which we hold about the basic make-up of the
world. James Sire, The Universe Next Door.
A world view answers:

-
-
-
-
-
-

   Post Modernism
   A bias against and rejection of Christianity. Why? _____ _____ to be
   _____.

2. Family breakdown and relational brokenness.
-
-
-

3. Media _____. (raised on a media diet; when the parental volume goes down,
the media volume goes up.)

4. The shrinking _____-_____ _____ _____ (mostly American, movies and MTV)

5. Pervasive _____.

6. Unrealistic _____, _____, and _____.
    -
    -
    -

7. Internet has made them:
    -
    -
    -
    -

8. Rate (time) of _____ has been significantly shortened. As a result, adolescents experience:
    -
    -
    -
    -
    -

9. Amorality and the crisis of _____ (i.e. honesty; 80% of Who's Who Among American High School Students admitted to cheating)

10. _____ driven (experience).

11. _____ and _____.

12. _____ _____.
     Longing for _____ and _____.
     Living the consequences of relational brokenness.
     They will encounter their own relational difficulties.

13. _____-_____.

14. Materialistic. (avg. expendable cash per week is $____) according to Teenage Research

15. Concerned with _____.

16. Deeply interested in _____ _____.
    - Looking for things that _____
    - Looking for _____
    - Looking for _____

17. Hopeful?

Our Response

1. Take a look in the mirror.
    -
    -
    -

2. Understand the place that _____ must hold in life.

3. Serve as a _____

4. Use _____ and _____ _____.

5. Relationships.
    What do they want most in a relationship?
    -
    -
    -
    -
    -
    -
    -

6. Aggressive relationships with the _____ and _____.

7. Know the culture. (_____-_____-_____)

8. Media _____ and _____.

9. Model and discuss _____. (getting along with others)

10. _____ _____ in the context of unconditional love.

11. Slow down.

12. Establish _____ _____. (i.e. work but not to get excessive lifestyle)

13. Promote _____ involvement.

14. _____-___ involvement.

15. Deliberate effort to _____ them into the _____.

16. For those in ministry:
   - _____ (coming together of the generations)
   - _____ (experiential)
   -

17. Patience.

18. Prayer.

(adapted from Walt Mueller, Center for Parent-Youth Understanding)

CONTACTING

<u>Contacting</u>

I. To Be _____ (by students)

      A. Goal is to be _____
      B. To be _____
      C. To be a part of the _____/_____/_____ _____ _____
      D. Probably the most _____ _____ of contacting
      E. When this level is neglected, the _____ _____ _____

II. To Be _____ (by students)

      A. The relationships are _____
      B. We know the students by _____ and _____ _____ ____
      C. We have had the _____ ____ _____

III. To Be _____(by students)

      A. The relationship has _____
      B. Communication has _____

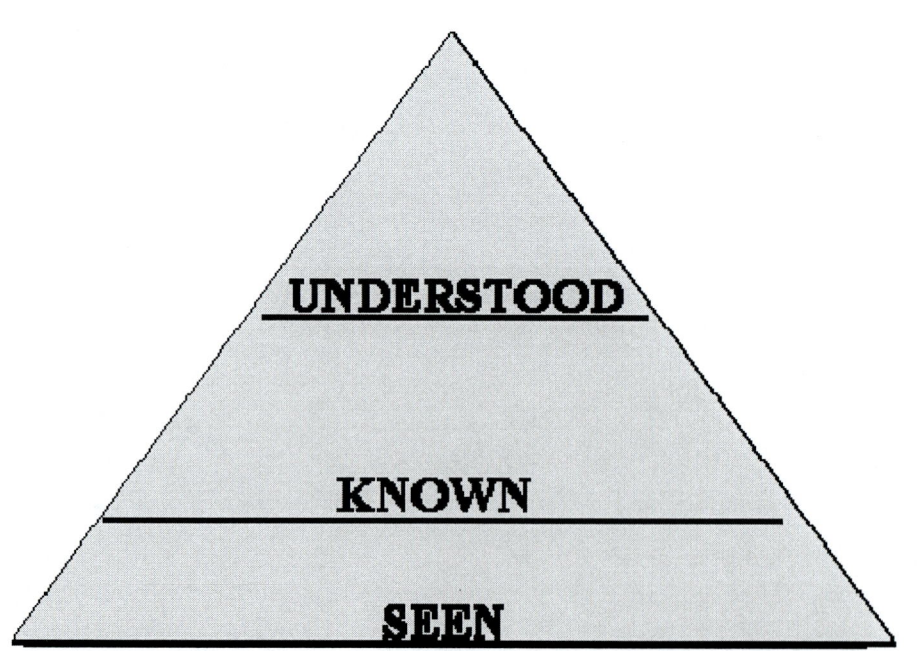

Myths about Contacting

1. Some people are just _____ at _____-I find it tough.

2. My campus is _____.

3. I'm _____ _____ to go on campus.

4. I'm afraid to ruin a relationship and tell a student about Jesus.

5. The _____ _____ _____ is too slow.

6. I'm too old to _____ ____ _____.

7. I don't _____ _____ ____ _____.

Who Are You in the Contact Work Process

How do you _____ _____?

How do you want _____ _____ _____?

How do you want to be recognized in the community?

Do you know where the students you are trying to reach are hanging out?

What are their _____, their _____?

What is _____ to _____?

How do they _____ _____ _____ _____?

Do you _____ _____ "_____"?

Do you know how to move among them in such a way that they are _____ _____ _____ _____?

What is Contact Work?

1. It is _____ the _____ to be _____ and _____.
2. It is _____ a _____ of _____.
3. It is _____ with _____ _____ _____ _____.
4. It is _____ and _____ a _____.
5. It is _____ _____ _____ for _____.
6. It is "_____ _____."
7. It is _____ the _____ ____ ____ _____ in _____ _____.

Why Do Contact Work?

1. The Scriptural Basis
   a.
   -
   -
   -

   b. Purpose of Contact Work
      We go to young people for the _____ _____ that _____
      _____ to _____ (Luke 19:10).
      Contact work reminds us of _____ _____ _____ _____
      _____. If it weren't for Him, we would _____ _____ in some
      comfortable setting with friends our own age.

"Jesus will not allow true religion to exist in comfortable little circles of its own. The new quality of life is love in action, and that may mean coping at firsthand with the difficult, the messy, and the unpleasant." *JB Phillips*

Personal Preparation

1. Our _____ with _____ is _____.
2. Have a '_____ _____'
3. Don't _____
4. _____ _____ and _____ should be carefully observed

Neighborhood/School Research

1. Get to _____ the _____.
      a. _____ of _____
      b. _____ of _____ _____
      c. _____, _____, and _____ background of the school
      d. Find out _____ the _____ _____ are (read the school paper or yearbook)
      e. Learn as _____ _____ as _____ (Keep a list)

Listening Skills

1. What you are communicating:
-_____ _____
-_____: facing square
Appropriate _____ (remember that each of us has a _____ _____ of what
an _____ _____ to sit or stand from another person. Don't _____ on a
person's personal space.)
      Leaning forward, if seated

2. Make concrete observations concerning _____ (_____ _____).
Basic responses like, '_____ _____ _____,' are OK but don't _____ _____
_____. This could be threatening.

3. Listening to _____ _____ is what observing is to non-verbal messages.

4. The major elements in listening are _____ _____ _____ _____ _____
and _____ on the facts and feelings contained therein.
5. A useful technique is the _____ _____.
      -_____ on hearing every word, and how it was said
-_____ what you have heard..."He said he felt 'such a way' about 'such a
thing.'"

6. If you are to listen effectively, you must work at _____ _____-_____.
_____ first, _____ later.

7. Often, feelings are only implied, whether by _____ _____ _____, _____
_____ _____, or non-verbal messages, so you may have to say, 'he appeared to be...'

15 Ways to Remember Names

1. Say the name _____.

2. Use the name frequently in the _____.

3. Ask a _____ using the name. ("Steve, how did you hear about our group?")

4. Say the name in your conversation _____.

5. _____ the name to someone you knew previously or to a place.

6. Take _____ _____ of them, write their names on the back of the pictures, and use them as flash cards.

7. Look closely and attentively at them as they speak and try to find _____ features about them.

8. Do something _____ with them. You always remember someone more when you are laughing and having fun!

9. When all else fails, give them _____ that are appropriate for them or sound like their names (keep this to yourself, unless it is edifying)

10. Ask for _____ information. (check for I.D.)

11. _____ the name with someone else you know with that name.

12. Study the student's _____ while you are being introduced.

13. Ask _____ to help you remember, and care; we remember what's important to us.

14. _____ the name down (on your hand, card, or scrap paper). The act of writing will help you retain it.

15. Ask students to _____ you on it.

f. Follow the _____ _____ in the _____ _____

g. Check to see _____ ____ _____ _____ might be sympathetic to a campus ministry

h. Learn any _____ _____ for _____ ____ _____

i. Get the _____ _____ of _____/_____

j. Find out _____ _____ _____ are at the school

k. Be aware of any _____ _____ _____
_____/_____/_____

l. Consider a _____/_____ with _____ _____

2. Have Christian people _____ for _____ _____.

3. Public relations contacts

a. Let _____ _____ _____ _____ know of your work.

b. Contact _____ _____
Be positive, supportive, and open to them.
Answer questions re: _____, _____, _____ _____,
_____, _____, etc.

c. Find out what other _____ or _____ are at work with high school students

-
-

d. Carefully _____ with _____ of _____ as to future plans

e. Get to know _____ _____, _____, etc. as _____, so they understand why you are there

<u>Guiding Thoughts in Contact Work</u>

1. Keep clearly in mind that our goal is that every young person should have the _____ to see and hear about our _____ of Hope.
2. We must be aware of _____ _____ within _____ _____.
3. Many times the Holy Spirit will lead you to students who don't seem to be "_____ _____" and often they will turn out to be our "_____ _____."
4. REMEMBER-You _____ Christ before students. You do not have to always be in with the socially '___ _____.' Spend quality time with all sorts of students and _____ _____.

<u>Three Levels of Contact Work</u>

1. Being seen at _____ _____ and wherever students are.
2. _____ with a _____. (If he goes on just 'hanging around', suspicions will grow as to his purposes.) We must remember to look at things from their point of view and _____ to _____ about things that are of _____ to them.
3. Enjoying _____ with students.

<u>When Do We Contact?</u>

1.
2.
3.

<u>General Suggestions and Principles for Contacting</u>

1. Practice the _____ of _____ _____.

2. Look for ways to _____ _____ _____
    A.
    B.
    C.

3. Do not attempt to '____ _____ ____ _____ _____.' Students need to see _____ _____ _____.

4. Seek to know others _____ ____ _____ _____.

5. Do not _____ _____ _____ into certain social situations, parties, or group discussions where you would not be welcome.

6. _____ _____ _____ of _____ _____. (This is the most dangerous kind of _____.)

7. Be careful about _____ _____ _____ of _____ _____ (athletic, scholastic, etc.).

8. Be _____.

       Don't try to impress with _____ or _____ _____.

       You don't have to be a _____, _____, or _____.

9. _____ _____ about _____ _____ when in conversation with high schoolers.

10. Ask God for a _____ _____ in _____ _____.

11. Be _____.

       Don't work too hard at being friendly (_____ _____, _____ _____).

12. Develop a _____ ____ _____. Find what fits you best.

13. Be _____. Expect to change your pace from time to time.

14. _____ _____ _____ _____ __ _____ _____ (students & staff).

15. Seek to gain friendships with ____ _____ ____ _____. Need to spend time with the 'chiefs' as well as the tribe.

16. _____ and _____ are _____.

17. Have a _____ _____ for _____ _____.

18. Pray for those you _____ _____ or _____ ____ _____.

19. Contact work is _____ _____.

20. Realize contact work is _____ with _____ in a way that Jesus identified with people.

21. Keep in mind that every relationship _____ _____ _____.

22. Be a person of _____ (II Cor. 6:3-10)

23. Do not _____ _____ to _____ and keep them for your _____ _____.

24. Contact while you are away. (_____, _____, etc.)

Five Reasons to Phone/Text a Student

1. Because something random reminded you of that person

2. Because you noticed a student wasn't there

3. Because you saw him/her taking great steps of faith or serving

4. To say thanks for something you saw a student do

5. To follow up on a previous conversation- letting the student know you remember

Questions to Ask Before I Leave the Car

1. Is the Spirit of Christ _____ and _____ ____ _____ _____? (Col. 1:27; Gal. 2:20; II Cor 2:15)

2. What is it about contact work that is _____ ____ ____? (Phil. 4:13; II Cor. 12:10; II Chron. 16:9)

3. What is it about contact work that is _____ ____ ____? (Eph. 3:7-9)

4. Who else will go to be Jesus to students ___ __ ____ ____ ___? (Ezek. 22:30)

5. Do I have a plan for where __ _____ ___ and what ___ _____ ____? (Acts 19:21-22)

6. How do I overcome the _____ ___ _____ as I leave the car and go in? (Luke 22:41-43)

7. What are my goals as a "relational minister"?
   - Will I _____ ____ _____ _____?
   - Will I _____ ____ _____ ___ ____?
   - Will I _____ ____ ____?
   - Will I _____ ___ _____ ____ _____?
   - Will I _____ _____ __ _____ _____?
   - Will I _____ ____ _____?
   - Will people _____ _____ ___ ____ _____?
   - Will I _____ ___ _____ _____?
   - Will I _____ _____ __ __ _____ _____?
   - Will my _____ ____ ___ _____ ___ _____-_____?
   - Will I _____ ___ ___ ?
   - Will God ___ _____ ____ _____ ___?

Fears in Doing Contact Work

1. The students will _____ us.
2. We as leaders won't know _____ ___ _____ or won't know what to _____ about.
3. The students will think we are _____.
4. We won't know how to _____ the _____ below the surface
5. We won't know how to ___ _____; we will feel _____-_____ or try to _____ someone else.
6. The students won't notice us if we are _____.
7. We will make a fool of ourselves or _____ _____ to ourselves, especially if we are outgoing.
8. We will _____ names of those we have met.
9. The students will think we are _____ and why we are here.

How Do We Overcome These Fears

1. Don't _____ _____ _____ (Students are looking for _____ _____ and healthy _____ _____ that they can _____, _____, and _____ ___).
2. _____ _____ in the One who calls you to those students.
3. You are still _____ _____ ___ _____ _____ (II Corinthians 4:7).
4. As for what to talk about, the key is to remember to _____ _____ _____. Ask things that the _____ _____ _____ _____ _____ (their sport, family, friends, job, etc.).
5. Remember to be a _____ _____. Ask _____ or _____-_____ questions.
6. Demonstrate an _____ of _____ and making students feel special.
7. Always let students know that you are at _____ because ___ _____.
8. Demonstrate _____ in practical ways.
9. _____, go _____ with a handful of students and _____ with many students. There are always new students to meet.
10. Never forget the importance of these aspects of contact work:
     -
     -
     -
     -

Things to Encourage in Students[2]

♦ Sense of Humor
♦ Determination
♦ Willingness to take a risk
♦ Choice of Friends
♦ Faithfulness
♦ Enthusiasm
♦ Loud voice
♦ Creative use of words
♦ Ability to deny ever using those creative words
♦ Ability to laugh at themselves
♦ Self control in not laughing at you
♦ Manners
♦ Precision during a food fight
♦ Willingness to clean up after a food fight
♦ Ability to survive on little sleep
♦ Ability to keep you from getting any sleep at all
♦ Willingness to baby-sit your kids
♦ Willingness to baby-sit your kids without pay
♦ Smile
♦ Ability to forgive others
♦ Ability to forgive you for kicking them out of Sunday School
♦ Willingness to stick around and clean up after events
♦ Positive, happy heart
♦ Flexibility
♦ Honesty
♦ Ability to … (edit a video, act, sing, play, etc.)
♦ Heart for prayer, missions, others, etc.
♦ Love for their friends
♦ Support of their parents
♦ Willingness to learn
♦ Ability to listen
♦ Perception of details
♦ Ability to make good decisions

---

[2] Youthworker, March/April 2002, "Relational Basics, How to Develop Relationships with Students," Doug Fields. P. 20-24.

◆ Street smarts
◆ Willingness to ask questions
◆ Pursuit of God
◆ Belief in the underdog
◆ Change of underwear
◆ Humility
◆ Ability to make others feel comfortable
◆ Quick wit
◆ That they're trustworthy
◆ That they speak kind words
◆ That they work hard
◆ That they trust God
◆ That they take steps of faith
◆ Their posture

Words to Use with Students[3]

I believe in you
You can do it
Don't give up
Great Idea!
You're a good thinker
I value your input
Got a breath mint?
Have you talked with him/her about it?
What do your parents think?
I'm confident in you'll make a good decision.
What do you like about him/her?
What are the potential consequences?
What do you think God is teaching you?
You're awesome!
What do you like about yourself?
What do you think I should do?
Will you pray for me?
Tell me more about that.
How do you think he/she feels?
What have you got to lose?
I loved your effort
You're a good friend
That's a perfectly normal thought/struggle.
What did you learn?
Ready to try?
Thanks for listening.
Thanks for helping
Want to come with me?
I'm listening
Huh? Did you say something?
What's your name again?

---

[3] Youthworker, March/April 2002, "Relational Basics, How to Develop Relationships with Students," Doug Fields. P. 20-24.

CAMPUS CLUB MEETING

The Campus Club

Introductory comments:

1. Usually held on a _____ in a _____ _____, such as a house of one of the students.
2. The leadership team is made up of people _____ _____ _____ _____ and want to express the Gospel of Christ.
3. A campus club leadership team has a great opportunity to _____ and _____ ____ or so _____ _____ a school year.

Primary Considerations:

1. Campus clubs are geared ____ _____ and _____ _____ _____. Nothing is _____ or _____ since Christ does not Himself.
2. The "____ ____ _____" of a club are all a part of the ____-_____ communication of Christ.
3. The leadership team helps set the _____ of Christ's love.
4. When students leave your club, they should feel _____ _____ about the time they were there.

Preliminary Considerations:

1. A campus club meeting features "_____ _____."
2. Typically, in _____ _____, the meeting lasts an hour. In _____ and _____ _____, the evening may involve recreational and social activities and as a result, last an evening. If home is a place for some students to "escape" from, they will want to stay ____ _____ _____ _____.
3. The program should _____ _____ and not '_____.'
4. The meeting is designed to _____ _____ _____ to Christ. It should not become a _____ ____ _____ _____ _____.
5. It should be _____ ___ _____ _____ in the school or community (including those who tend to be "_____ _____.").
6. Leaders should make every opportunity to _____ with _____ _____. Your campus club should be viewed as an _____ ____ ____ _____.
7. The campus club should not _____ with _____ _____ or become a "_____" of its own.
8. Information, both _____ and _____, must be given to parents.
9. You should attempt to meet on a _____ _____, the same night of the week. Continually shifting or canceling club will only confuse students.
10. Leaders should be _____ with their club program.
11. Keeping _____ _____ ___ _____ will help future contacting.
12. Leaders must exercise care in the _____ of _____ _____, as well as watch over the conduct of young people before and after the club meeting. _____ must be replaced and proper apologies given.

13. Leaders should pray and work towards to a balance of _____ and _____ in the club.
14. The message should be the _____ ____ _____ _____.

Atmosphere of a Campus Club:
1. Should be _____ and _____.
2. Envision the _____ ____ _____ flowing through you to each student there.
3. Let students know ____ _____ _____ _____ _____.
4. Give students as much _____ _____ _____.
5. Keep things _____.
6. Team leaders _____ _____ _____ _____ and give the 'up front' leader their _____ _____ (this attitude is contagious).

Traditional Ingredients of a Campus Club Meeting:
1.
2.
3.
4.
5.

Leadership Responsibilities Before a Campus Club Meeting:
1. Schedule and conduct a weekly team meeting for

    -

    -

    -

    -

2. Arrange for a home, usually running _____ _____ ____ _____ _____.
3. Make final preparations of the _____ of _____ in the club meeting.
4. Prepare the _____.
5. Arrive _____ enough to:

    -

    -

    -

    -

6. Make sure leaders are bringing _____ _____/_____/
    _____.
7. Ask permission to _____ or _____ _____/
    _____/_____/_____.
8. When appropriate, have students _____ _____.
9. _____ _____ at the door.
10. No student should leave without a _____ _____ ____
    _____.

During the Campus Club Meeting:

1. Be ____ _____ of all that goes on, making sure of _____.
2. Deliver the message _____ and _____.
3. Be sensitive to _____ _____ to every part of the meeting.
4. Help make the club ____ _____ (i.e. latecomers, discipline, etc.)
5. Be in prayer for other leaders and the students, especially _____ _____ _____.
6. Take part in the meeting with _____.
7. When you are not up front, _____ _____ ____ _____, especially new ones.
8. Be most _____ and _____ with the one who is up front.
9. Make yourself available to anyone ____ _____ ____ _____ _____.
10. Use _____ in your campus clubs.

Why Crowd Breakers

1. Students need something to '_____ ____ _____' among themselves.
2. Students are naturally _____ _____.
3. They _____ _____ between the leader and the students.
4. Crowd breakers can be great _____ _____.

The How of Crowd Breakers

1. Surprise the _____-not _____.
    - _____ _____ the activity
     - Go through it _____ _____ _____
2. Choose the _____ _____
    - Lively, responsible people
3. Program _____
    - Move from the "_____" to the _____
4. Give some thought to _____
    - How much space will you need?
5. Work on your _____
6. Sell it!
    -

7. If it's not working, _____ ____!
8. Be wise and be harmless
    -

    -

    -

9. Think up ____ _____.
10. Don't be afraid to _____ _____ _____.

Endless Word

Have a group form a circle. One person says a word and then counts to five at a moderate speed. Before this person says five, the person to their right has to say another word that begins with the last letter of the word just said. This continues on around the circle until someone is unable to come up with a word before the count of five. Two misses and the person is out of the game (or one miss if you have a very large group). If it is the person's first miss, she starts it again with any word. No one is allowed to repeat a word that has already been spoken. If no one is being eliminated, have them count to five more rapidly. Or if everyone is getting out, have them count to 10 or 15 instead of five. This game can be quiet lively and you will soon find out who is out to get the person next to them.
Brian Scuffler

Question and Answer Game

Hand out plain cards and pencils to everyone in the group. Divide into two teams. Have everyone on one team write a question beginning with how, such as, "How do you peel a prune?" Everyone on the other team will write an answer beginning with by, such as "By using pinking shears." Collect the cards, keeping them in two separate piles. Read a question first and then an answer. Random reading will produce hilarious results.

Making Appointments

You should consider making an appointment with a student:

1. If you notice fairly _____ _____ _____

   -

   -

   -

   -

2. If _____ or _____ _____ _____

   -

   -

   -

   -

3. If they seem too _____ or _____

4. If they are too _____ to be _____ _____ and to _____ _____

5. If you would just like to _____ _____ _____

6. If the _____ _____ prompts you

7. To check out rumors that they might be experiencing a problem

   -

   -

   -

8. In response to a referral from another _____, a _____, a _____, _____ _____, _____, etc.

How Do You Control a Crowd of Young People with an Unlimited Supply of Energy?

1. Forecasting potential problems

    A. The _____ _____ (Is it the right size for your crowd?)

    B. _____ (Will certain students who have a history of causing trouble be there?)

    C. Attention span

        1. Is it short?

        2. Is the program designed to hold their attention? (variety/fast paced)

        3. Spot possible lulls.

    D. _____ _____ (Which games lend towards rowdiness?)

    E. The _____ (Are staff mixed among the students?)

    F. The _____ _____ (Is it interesting?)

2. Other Considerations

    A. Careful _____

    B. Clear _____ _____

    C. Fast _____

    D. Determination to _____ _____

    E. Willingness to let students get away with a certain amount of _____ within your limits

    F. Avoid _____ _____ ___ _____ _____

    G. If at all possible, get with them _____

Small Group Suggestions

1. The group must meet the _____ of _____.
  - There must be _____ ____ ____ for the individual teen

2. Groups must be based on _____ _____.
  - Guys
  - Girls
  - What Does the Bible Have to Say About…
  - Skaters
  - Team Athletes
  - Freshmen, Sophomores, Jrs., Srs.

3. Groups should have some _____ ____ _____
  - Enhances group interaction
  - Quiet, compliant students
  - Outgoing students

4. The group should gain a _____ from the students to be a part of the group
  -
  -

5. The group has to be _____
  - No rude or vicious comments
  - Express feelings without attacking others in the group

6. The _____ and _____ of group meetings needs to be clearly understood.
  - Don't assume anything
  - Where
  - What time
  - Transportation

THE BASICS OF SMALL GROUP LEADERSHIP

1. _____ - eye contact, listening posture, everyone at the same level.

2. Communication guidelines - no _____, _____ when someone else is talking, everyone gets an _____ to participate.

3. Purpose of the group -_____ _____ _____ _____?

4. _____ - be there unless there is a death in the family (your own), be on time, stay until the end, contribute.

5. Learn to listen actively -_____, _____, _____.

6. Learn to ask _____ questions (cannot be answered with yes or no) such as "How", "what do you think of...," "what would it be like if ..."

7. Be willing to _____ the group when it goes off-track.

8. Be willing to gently _____ members who are _____.

9. Develop and share _____ within the group.

10. Build group _____.

11. _____ what the group has accomplished (closure) and make people aware of the next meeting time and place.

UPFRONT LEADERSHIP SKILLS

Youth workers can learn skills to improve their ability to provide effective leadership to groups of teens. Good leadership begins with an understanding of what it means to be a great leader and a willingness to take some risks!! The best song leaders are not necessarily the most musical and the funniest leaders in a skit are not necessarily those who have the best humor. They have learned how to establish leadership from upfront and how to create an atmosphere of participation in music and laughter. The tips below can be applied to all upfront situations, such as, explaining a game, leading singing, speaking about Christ, doing a skit, etc.

- Begin by seeing yourself as the_____of the group

- Take _____ quickly and make it happen - don't wait for the perfect moment

- Think about how the group _____ you and focus on presenting yourself with a leadership presence:
    -
    -
    -
    -

- Lead with your _____ - speak loudly and clearly, project to the students at the back
- Lead with your _____ - movement, hands, face
- Use a _____ that students would feel comfortable with, ie, don't sound like a parent or a teacher, speak to the students who seem most uncomfortable with authority
- Plan ahead the things you want to say, ie, how to explain a complicated game, how you will introduce a speaker, etc.
- Make it a goal to _____ - practice in front of a mirror, ask for feedback
  Use humor!! Have fun!! Project _____!!

As a youth worker, you have the ability to help kids experience what you believe they should experience as a part of God's Kingdom. If you want them to feel accepted, if you want them to laugh a lot, if you want them to think God is interesting and exciting, if you want them to experience excellence in music and humor.... you can take hold of any situation, do your part and lead it towards these goals by the example you set and the atmosphere you create.

HELPFUL IDEAS BASIC TO EVERY EVENT

Leaders focus on _____ ... not other leaders

Be aware of what is going on in the _____ _____

Lead by _____. Get involved.

_____ people around. Help them _____

_____ in the crowd. Mix and blend into the crowd

Give attention to _____ person and respond. Cooperate

Provide leadership. Move people

Think. Plan _____. Communicate.

Consider carefully _____ events happen

Use _____ creatively and wisely

Keep looking for ways to _____ names

Use mixers and games that help people get involved immediately

Use _____ time for getting better aquatinted

Write out names of young people after every event ... it helps you remember

Every leader is responsible for the _____ of each event

MUSIC

There is something special about music. It is no surprise then that one of the tools we use in relational ministry is music. But today group singing is something to flee from for many students, especially guys. We need to be both current and cautious in using certain historical tools which may turn students off. Most students who dislike campus club meetings list singing as the chief reason. So take a regular pulse of the students in your program and experiment - sing-a-long tapes, karaoke, electric guitars and drum machines can help to make singing more acceptable to "cool" students.

We need to be sharp in this department. Therefore, plan and practice your music prayerfully so it is not merely a preliminary to get "over with," so the message can be given.

1. **Purpose**
   A. Why have music in campus club meetings?
      1. It_____.
      2. It is _____.
      3. It _____.
      4. It _____.
      5. It _____, breaks down barriers.
      6. It presents a _____.
      7. It _____ with where students are.

   B. Why *not* have music in club?
      1. Some students in group _____ like to sing.
      2. Keeps some students _____ who would otherwise come.
      3. Intimidates and embarrasses students who are _____.
      4. Group singing _____ to some youth cultures.
      5. Leadership team may lack people with gifts needed to make it effective.

   C. POINT - As a leadership team, prayerfully determine the best Course of action for your ministry in terms of singing.

CREATING A JR HIGH/MIDDLE SCHOOL PROGRAM

Beginning Considerations:

1) **Relationship With/To High School Ministry**

    A— _____ (ie. events, leadership, committee, teams)? If yes, how will you split them and distinctly promote them?

    B—How will the High School and Jr High School program _____and/or _____each other?
1. How often will you meet?
2. Will you do music?
3. All-city events or individual schools?

    C—How can you involve _____in the Jr High ministry? High-schoolers themselves?

2) **Evaluate Resources**

    _____needs:
A— Who is interested in and would make a good Jr High leader?

    B— What parents do you know and how could you involve them?

    _____:
C—Who is available to give these leaders ongoing support and aining? What kind of training will they need? Can we provide it?

    _____Contacts:
D—Who could provide prayer support? Administrative "ins" to schools?

From the above - Determine the best time and place to start.

YEARLY CALENDAR:

Come up with a year-long plan for Jr. High ministry in your community. Include:
1) Recruitment and Training of Leaders
2) Event and Camp Schedule
3) Message Plan

STARTING A NEW MINISTRY

A. WHICH SCHOOL, OR NEIGHBORHOOD, IF THERE IS A CHOICE?

1. Where you already have _____ interest, particularly _____ interest.

2. Where you already have _____ _____ upon which to build.

3. Contact _____ and other _____ (Campus Life or Young Life, for example) to see who has a current outreach program at the targeted school or community. If there is already a productive program, either offer to work together or move on to another school or community. (You should *never* seek to compete!)

4. A strategic school, or neighborhood, as far as _____ leaders are concerned, i.e., close to a college campus.

5. If possible, start in a school which, if the word spreads, will open doors to other schools more easily.

B. PRELIMINARIES -- Ground Work

Calling should be done upon school officials, ministers, etc. If possible, have a _____ _____ who is active in the community open the door for these contacts and go along with you. This procedure enhances _____.

C. SELLING THE IDEA TO STUDENTS -- This may be done in several ways:

1. Take students to see another _____ _____, at the invitation of that club. Check first always with the leaders of the existing club so they can warmly greet those who visit.

2. Use the _____.

3. Have a _____ in which the campus club is introduced by the leader and students already active in campus ministry somewhere, show slides of the camping program, etc.

4. Encourage notable, well-known personalities to come to an introductory meeting and give their _____ and encouragement.

5.   Have a party, or barbecue, complete with games and entertainment, followed by a _____ of the campus ministry idea.

6.   Perhaps a high school assembly for a staff speaker could open some ideas for how to proceed strategically.

7.   The most effective way to sell is to explain the campus club or event which gives the ministry its identity. Have fun doing it, but then make sure they know the choice is theirs to make. The "_____ ____ _____" approach is usually the best.

ENCOURAGING DECISIONS

Campus ministry leadership should be determined not to use embarrassing "button-hole" techniques. Yet, we must keep in mind the young person who might respond with a more directed and guided chance to trust Christ at a campus club. We do not need to wait for camps or special meetings to expect students to make their commitment to Jesus Christ. If we give a closing prayer we may help them phrase their own prayer of faith. Leaders should be available to students who might want to talk. We must make it as easy as possible to see us. We may want to encourage them publicly to come, letting them know we would like to help in any way possible. A direct question from the leader is in order with those we know very well, such as, "What do you think about all of this?"

It could happen at any time or place when a leader senses the young person wants help in meeting Christ in a personal way.

WHAT DO STUDENTS WANT OUT OF LIFE?

. Students want to be_____; they want to get to know themselves better.

. Students want to _____ new people, especially those of the opposite _____.

. Students need to feel _____ and important.

. Students want to _____ with one another, _____ with one another, get to know one another.

. Students want to hear about Christ in ways that they can _____.

. Students expect to have _____ and be surprised.

. Students want to be challenged in their _____.

. Students need to be _____ by one another.

. Students **don't like** -- _____.
  -- _____ of club.
  -- Another social event.

The Essentials of Planning a Spring Break Trip

1. _____

    Consider:
        Length of Spring Break
        Travel Time
        Costs
        Destination

2. _____

    Where you are staying
        Hotels
        Homes
        Tents
        Camps/Conference Centers
    Who is going to feed you?
    What are you going to eat?
        Quality/quantity can make or break the spirit of a trip
        Kids eat on their own
    What you are going to do?
        Tourist Attractions
    Service/Work Projects
    Who should go? (Age/grade/school)

3. _____

    Must sell this idea to church leadership, parents, kids, schools
    Brochure
    Promote in school
    Videotape
    Someone who's been there
    Display

4. _____

    September
    February
    One month before
    The week before
    The day before

5. _____ _____ and more _____

    Release forms
    Medical forms
    Identification

6. _____

    Students pay entire fee
    Students engage in fundraising
    Great opportunity to get to know kids
    Manage the money (some cash; mostly traveler's checks; dummy wallet; money belt; keep receipts)

7. _____

    Getting there
    Getting around when you're there

8. _____ _____

    A time for fun (don't need a lot)
    A time to let students know of the next day's schedule (HINT: Give them one day at a time)
    A time for challenge
    A time to present the Gospel

9. _____

    No whining
    Be flexible
    No pairing off
    No drinking/illegal drugs
    Be on time
    No skipping meetings
    Always be in groups of three (preferable with at least one guy in group)

10. _____ _____

    Location and Date of Departure/Arrival
    Phone #'s
    Payment Schedule
    Form Schedule
    Q/A time
    Video Clip
    What to Bring List

What Not to Bring List

11. _____
      Have a reunion
      Have a photo party
-Renews friendships
        -Builds excitement for next year
        -Great PR in the school
      Have students fill out an evaluation form

<u>Camping</u>

I. DEFINITION OF CAMPING

Camping is defined as <u>any time a leader or leaders take students out of their normal environment.</u>

II. ELEMENTS OF CAMPING

A. <u>Counselor-Centered</u>, or more simply defined, "Relationships." The whole of any camping program we put together should center on the relationship between a leader and students. Not only does that relationship give us the credibility for everything else we do with the students, it serves as the model or basis for discussing what it means to have a relationship with Christ. Especially in today's world, we need to realize that a stable relationship between a leader and a young person may very well be the only stable relationship in that student's life. It is next to impossible to understand the concept of a relationship with Christ if we have no good relationships in our lives to serve as models. We need to ensure in our own minds and programs that the relationships between leaders and students is foremost in how we plan trips. The things we do with students are only effective in our ministry in so much as they (1) build those relationships or (2) use those relationships to convey a message to the students.

B. <u>Alternative Environment</u>. This refers to that process of taking students out of their routine environment (especially out of town) to a setting which is unique to them. This enhances the stopping of students long enough to hear the gospel. Although we are not advocating that students move when they become Christians, when presenting the Christian faith to non-Christians we are basically talking about a complete change in that person's world -- a change into a different personal and spiritual environment. Therefore, it is sometimes helpful to pull students into a neutral physical setting to more fully allow them to take an objective look at their own lives and make decisions based on a "new" picture of what their life could look like.

C. <u>Message.</u> Here referring to the verbal proclamation of the gospel. This can take many forms (e.g., talks, Bible study, testimonies, etc.) and should be consistent with our emphasis on relationships. We do not build someone's trust in order to cram something down his or her throat. Rather, our proclamation should be a verbalization of that which the students have already experienced through their relationships with leaders. We describe a relationship with Christ which is the reason they notice a difference in their leaders' lives, and which is consistent with the relationship they have experienced with their leaders. The other important thing to note here is that the speaker, or presenter, needs to see his or her role as secondary to the leader or counselor. The speaker is simply putting into words what the leader is fleshing out for the kids, and it is the leader's responsibility to ensure that the students understand and contemplate the message, which leads to the fourth major piece of the puzzle.

D. Processing. Processing takes people a step beyond giving them information and asking them to think about it. Here people are given the chance to talk about the subject, ask questions, look at any significance it has in their own life, and especially discover new insights by listening to themselves talk as opposed to simply listening to someone else's ideas. Students today are overwhelmed with information. We need to make sure that we are doing more with the gospel than simply passing it on as another does in their diet of information. On the other hand, students today have very little chance to process all of their information (little time with parents, etc.). And we know that information alone does not change lives. It is only as that information is processed, sorted, and integrated that lives become changed. Our camping programs need to include a mechanism to process that which is presented to students. In most settings this can be accomplished through small groups under well-trained leadership, hence a need to train people to put less emphasis on good speaking and more on good group leading skills. We stand a much better chance today of winning a student to Christ through mediocre speaking and great processing than through articulate, polished speaking and poor or no group processing.

III. A DESIGN FOR AN OUTREACH CAMPING EXPERIENCE:

A. Christ-Centered in Origin

The camper should leave the camp in awe of the facilities, impressed
With the food, struck by the program, but most importantly touched by the person of Christ.

Every aspect of the camping experience should honor and point to God. This must begin long before the camper arrives.

The facilities should reflect Christ. They need not be overwhelming in beauty but should be well taken care of and perhaps even understated so as not to draw away from both the God-created surroundings and the message of Christ during the camp. It is not the camp or staff we urge kids to remember, it's the Savior.

One of the toughest areas in which to be Christ-centered and yet one of the most critical is in the program. The role of the program is to provide a positive atmosphere for the presentation of the gospel. Humor, music, and enjoyable activities are the primary vehicles used to accomplish this task. In the lives of many non-Christian students, the humor they respond to, the music they enjoy, and the activities they engage in and declare as enjoyable are far from Christ-centered. The program director must often pioneer new ground in humor, music, and activities for these people. Unfortunately, some program directors do not take that risk and compromise a Christ-centered program for one that will get laughs and involvement from kids through vehicles the kids feel comfortable with. Music with questionable lyrics, humor that is destructive or suggestive, and activities that are distinctively worldly are the results of this compromise and Christ is lost in the shuffle. The program must strive to provide students with a very positive alternative to what they engage in day-to-day.

The program director should be a facilitator of fun and not the center of camper's attention. His or her position is one of high profile and every effort must be made to point the kids to Christ and not to human personalities.

The rest of the staff must follow suit. Work crew kids have a powerful impact on the kids in camp. For kids to see contemporaries working for Christ and not for money is an incredible message.

Everyone from assigned staff, to work crew, to property staff, to staff spouses is responsible to present Christ to the camper. Although that presentation may not be verbal in nature, actions and attitudes speak loudly and clearly to kids.

B. Relational in Nature

Camping must be a relational ministry. All year long, staff and volunteers spend time with students "on their own turf" to win their trust and ear. Camp should be no different.

Camping should be a Christian counselor's dream. Every aspect of the experience should enhance the counselor's ability to share and explain Christ to the camper.

The facilities should be large enough for campers to feel free in movement, but small enough so that staff and counselors can remain in touch and relational with the students. This can be a fine line.

There should be plenty of things for counselors to do at camp with students during free time. Counselors must be instructed in how to use this relational time with kids to firm up friendships or to use firm friendships to discuss

Christ. Facilities should also be built with relationships in mind. Large comfortable sitting areas and cabins conducive to conversation should be designed with relational evangelism as the goal.

Camping needn't be so hectic that relational ministry is thwarted. Many camps are so over-programmed that students and counselors have neither the time nor the energy to build or strengthen relationships. This is the fault of the program director. The camp needs to involve activities that build relationships and evangelism on the part of the counselor.

No matter how fine the facility or how perfect the schedule, if counselors are not doing their job, all is wasted. Counselors need to have been trained biblically and in methodology, and closely supervised and encouraged by the assigned staff. The role of the head counselor is to equip, encourage, and assist counselors in their monumental task of ministering to their students.

C. <u>Evangelism</u>

Students are at camp to hear about, and hopefully respond to Jesus Christ. A camp ministry does not run health resorts, athletic camps, or places to "just get away." Youth ministry is in evangelistic outreach camping. Evangelism should be of highest priority.

The most visible vehicle of evangelism is the camp speaker. This person will daily have the opportunity to present the Gospel to students. All should be excellent. The music, the humor, and all activities in club should pave the way for the climax - the gospel presentation. The presentation should be enjoyable, reasonable in length, and most importantly, clear in understanding. The series of messages should logically build upon one another with the Person of Christ, sin, the work of Christ, and personal appropriation included. The messages should be a springboard for counselor/camper discussion and it is often helpful for the speaker to pose questions to be discussed in cabin time.

Although the speaker is the "up front" communicator of the gospel, the counselor "in the trenches" with students remains the primary evangelist. The counselor clarifies, expounds, and personalizes the speaker's message and it is often the counselor who actually leads the camper to Christ. Evangelism begins when counselor meets student, continues to camp, through camp, and often after camp until a student accepts Christ. If a student rejects Christ, evangelism continues. If a student meets Christ, discipleship begins. The counselor must not be afraid to cross that relational bridge he has built. He must cross that bridge with the Gospel of Christ.

D. Conclusion

Camping in its self is not holy. Yes, it has been used by God to produce holy results, but it is not sacred in and of itself. Youth ministries must be willing to constantly evaluate effectiveness and adapt camping approaches to see students won to Christ. That is our goal, to provide the most efficient and effective way for a leader to see his or her camper come to Christ.

Creative Camping Possibilities

1) **Hiking Trip**
   - take a group of 2 to 12 students
   - need 1 leader for each 5-6 students
   - go to anyplace out of town where you can hike with no one else around
   - program involves hiking and cooking
2) **Canoe Trip**
   - take a group of 6 to 15 students
   - need 1 leader for each 4 students
   - good idea to bring along an extra motor boat for food and emergencies
   - program involves canoeing and cooking and fun in the water
   - go to any large lake or river (if everyone has experience canoeing)
3) **Spelunking Trip**
   - take 2 to 10 students
   - take students who are not squeamish types and who like a physical challenge (it is hard work and you spend most of your time wet)
   - need one leader for each 2-3 students program involves exploring caves and cooking
   - often part of this camp involves a hike since few caves are accessible by road
   - you need to have along safety equipment and at least one experienced caver
4) **Rock Climbing Trips**
   - take 5 to 10 students
   - need one leader for every 2-3 students
   - program involves rock climbing, cooking, and relaxing in the sun
   - need to have all of the equipment (expensive) and all of the leaders need to know how to operate the climbing gear properly (no margin for error here)
5) **Bike Trips**
   - take 5 to 30 students
   - need 1 leader for every 5-6 students
   - program involves biking and exploring area
   - need to figure out if you want to bring your gear on the bike or have a base camp that you leave from every day
6) **Cabin Trip**
   - 5 to 10 students
   - 1 leader for each 5 students
   - program is walking around outside, and playing games inside
   - easy to do, need to borrow someone's cabin
7) **City Trip**
   - go to another city and spend a few days there (go to a hockey game, to the mall, visit another Young Life club or campaigners, or just hang out)
   - 2 to 10 students
   - 1 leader for each 4-5 students
   - program is hanging out at different places in the city
   - stay at someone's house (or a hotel if you're rich) and pay them for the food

THE MESSAGE

A. INTRODUCTION

1.   What we are about in campus ministry in all its fullness [John 10:10]
2.   How can we know God? By looking at Jesus Christ [John 1:14; Col. 1:15]

B. JESUS CHRIST

1.   His claims about Himself [John 6:35, John 8:12, John 14:6,9, John 10:30]
Who is He? [Matt. 8:27]

2.   Jesus cares for us when we are hurting - He is compassionate
[John 8:1-11, Luke 18:35-43, Mark 1:40-45, Mark 5:25—34]

3.   Jesus shows power over nature [Matt. 8:23—27]

4.   Jesus has power to forgive [Mark 2:1—12]

5.   Jesus accepts us as we are [Luke 15:1—10]

C. SIN

1.   Sin — what is it? Separation from God [Isaiah 53:6, Romans 3:23 (all have sinned... it is a universal problem), also John 8:1—11]
2.   Sin breaks God's heart [Luke 19:41,42]

3.   Sin results in death [Romans 6:23]

D. THE CROSS & RESURRECTION

1.   Jesus predicted his death [John 10:11]

2.   Jesus was guiltless [Luke 23:4, 20—22]

3.   Jesus died as a substitute: Story of Barabbas [Matt. 27:15—26]

4.   Jesus gave His life for ours as an act of love [John 15:13]

5.   Jesus rose from the grave: The Empty Tomb [John 20:1-18]

6.   Jesus' response to doubt: Story of Thomas [John 20:24-29]

E.   RESPONSE — HOW DO I BECOME A CHRISTIAN?

1. Jesus calls people to follow Him [Matt. 9:9]

2. Count the cost [Mark 10:17-22]

3. By decision [Rev. 3:20, John 1:12]

3. The gift of God [Romans 6:23]

Below is a brief description of a suggested message sequence:

1. **Introduction to the campus club:** What is the campus club all about? What will we be doing in the meetings? What will we be talking about? Why?

2. **God's Character:** Is there a God? If there is a God, what is He like?

3. **The Person of Jesus Christ:** The claims and credentials of Jesus.

4. **Human Need (Sin):** What is sin? How does sin affect relationships between us and God? Between us and each other? Between us and ourselves?

5. **The Work of Christ:** (cross and resurrection) What is the meaning of what Jesus did by dying on the cross and rising from the dead?

6. **Appropriation:** Why should we be committed to Jesus Christ? What does such commitment involve?

7. **The Christian Life:** What is it like to be in a relationship with Christ? What are the implications of our faith in a hurting world?

The Youth Center
(Drop-in center; coffee house, etc)

1. _____
        a. Near the school
        b. In the school
        c. A neutral sight
        d. Within the church facilities

2. _____ _____ _____
        a. Coffee house setting
        b. Gym setting
        c. Family room setting
        d. Pool/Games room setting

3. _____
        a. Determined by:
           -
           -
           -

        b. Elements
           -
           -
           -
           -
           -
           -

        c. Crossing the Bridge _____
           -Personal relationships
           -Corporate worship
           -Free nights with Bible Study to Follow
           -Small groups

4. _____ _____
        a. Start up costs   e. Church Budgeted
        b. Monthly costs   f. Community support
        c. Staff   g. Individual support
        d. Ownership/Leadership/Directors

VOLUNTEERS

The staff work is not merely a player, nor is he/she a playing-coach, but he/she is a general manager-playing coach. _____-ministry is what Jesus had in mind when he said, "A new command I give you: Love one another. As I have loved you, so you must love one another. By this all men will know that you are my disciples, if you love one another." (John 13:34,35) Building a team requires creating an _____ of love and support among the team members -this takes time. The best teams are the best of_____, they enjoy one another and they enjoy spending time with one another.

WHY PEOPLE DO NOT VOLUNTEER

1) They lack _____
2) They are _____
3) They lack _____
4) Fear of _____
5) Fear of _____
6) Fear of the _____

OUR RESPONSE to this
1) A _____ exposure to the task ("baby steps")
2) Steady _____
3) Modeling of _____
4) _____ is essential

A Training Program For Volunteers:

1) Identify the _____ to be completed
2) Identify the _____ and _____ needed to accomplish each task
3) Prioritize tasks according to overall impact
4) Match _____ with tasks
5) Determine _____ needs of volunteers based on the task they will be performing
6) Develop a training _____ that teaches the right kind of knowledge and the needed skills
7) Provide _____ training

PROBLEMS IN VOLUNTEERISM

1. _____. We must develop a training program; often watch people fail before they succeed, be frustrated and disappointed when important tasks are left undone, pick up the pieces ourselves. Wouldn't it have been easier just to do it ourselves? In the short term the answer is yes, but we need to take a long term view of ministry and of the development of people's potential.

2. _____. They may challenge some of our notions about how the work should be done; they may have more abilities in certain areas than we do; they may be different from our idea of a volunteer; they may be older or better than we are; we may not want to admit that we need help. If we have these types of insecurities we will be reluctant to recruit the brightest and the best; we will develop a narrow definition of a volunteer that will serve to build up our own self-image but not the work of the Kingdom of God.

3. _____. It has been said that "how you finish is more important than how you begin". A youth ministry can start with a great deal of excitement and promise led by one person, but if that one person leaves the ministry, there will be a heap of frustration and disappointment unless there are long term volunteers left to carry on the ministry.

4. _____ - to be a good leader and a poor delegator is a contradiction in terms. A delegate may be defined as "One sent and empowered" - both are necessary. Delegation will be effective when "delegates" know their authority and accountability. A delegate needs from the leader a high degree of clarity and access. At the same time the delegate must keep the leader informed. In the end, an honest evaluation of results, a vital part of personal growth, must follow. Proper delegation is essential to keeping volunteers involved long-term.

5. _____. It is important that we know what we are expecting a volunteer to do and be able to communicate that clearly.

TEN WRONG WAYS TO RECRUIT VOLUNTEERS

1. _____. Tell them that their job can be performed with minimum preparation without cutting into their free time and personal activities.
2. Talk about your _____ _____ - you know, the ones who carry their Bibles, sing out loud in church, and smile a lot.
3. Push the _____ and _____. Be sure to mention the ski vacation in the mountains and the celebrity they will meet after the next concert.
4. Show off your books, files and catalogues of _____ and _____. Tell them you have everything they need to do their job.
5. Tell the story of the student who turned from drugs to Jesus after a volunteer leader spoke to him. (Don't mention that it happened in another youth group.)
6. Explain that you and the Pastor have prayed together for the right leaders and that God has engraved their names in your hearts.
7. Talk about some of the _____ _____ you have received from other people who don't care enough for your students. If they know some of these people, mention them by name.
8. Remind them of the person who said "NO" to the opportunity and who was later involved in a tragic automobile accident. (Or illness, loss of job, death in the family, etc.)
9. Recruit through your _____ and _____. Let everyone know that you are looking for someone to volunteer, and give the job to the first person who responds.
10. _____ ____ _____. Tell people you don't think you can continue unless you get some more help. Then, even if no one volunteers to help the students, someone might volunteer to help you.

-John Hall
from *YOUTHWORKER*, Vol. II, No. IV, Winter 1986, p. 48.

RECRUITMENT

Sources of volunteers: kids in club, churches, parents, universities/colleges, other volunteers; committee members, announcements, mission's displays, adult camp, adult events, community Volunteer Bureau

Recruitment season: the best time to recruit volunteers is when there is no_____ _____.
If we can anticipate our needs well in _____ we will be able to fill them without a sense of panic. We live in busy times so in order to fill our committees we may need to ask people to be involved a year in advance; leaders should be approached in the spring for a fall involvement; in the summer for Christmas.

KEEPING VOLUNTEERS - a checklist
1. Give vision and _____ (high expectations).
2. Maximize their gifts through proper _____.
3. Say _____ _____ (see non-monetary rewards).
4. Communicate (_____).
5. Keep 'short' accounts.
6. Be friends - _____ attract people, _____ keep them.
7. Motivate through _____, _____, _____ and _____.

NON-MONETARY REWARDS
1. _____ recognition in front of the group.
2. Phone call/_____.
3. _____.
4. Sharing _____.
5. _____ _____ in a newsletter or church bulletin.
6. Remember _____ and _____.
7. Hold an "appreciation" _____/_____.
8. Hold a "leaders only" _____.
9. Provide free _____ for a night out or weekend away.
10. Write their pastor to _____ them.

**The team must commit itself as a group to loving each other.
Following is a list of ways this should be acted out.**

1. _____ (concerned for needs and available to meet them -
   Phil. 2:3, 4)
2. _____ (requiring honesty, sensitivity and confidentiality -
   James 5:16)
3. _____ (recognize and speak the others' worth and potential -
   I Thess. 5:11)
4. _____ (Eph. 5:21)
5. _____ (Matt. 18:15-17, II Tim. 4:2)
6. _____ (I John 5:14, 15; Matt. 18:20)
7. _____ (Col. 3:16)
8. _____

Top 10 Etiquette Points for Adults

- **Return calls and answer letters/emails/texts promptly.** Calls should be returned within 48 hours and letters within two weeks. If you cannot respond yourself within that time, have someone else do it for you. *Telephone etiquette:* When you call someone and your call-waiting signals, ignore it. You made the call, so you should give it priority. Be respectful of a person's schedule and obligations when choosing a time to call.

- **RSVP within one week to all invitations.** Go to an event when you have accepted...call ahead if you can't make it. If you accept an invitation and then fail to attend, call or write to apologize.

- **Introduce people properly and in a flattering way.** State the person's name clearly and correctly, as well as his/her title, occupation and city of residence if somewhere other than where you are. Also give their hobbies or interests, especially when they are similar to those of the person to whom you're making the introduction. And always introduce the less important or younger person to the more important or older.

- **Take care to use people's titles properly.** Doctors, judges, people of military rank and elected officials should always be addressed with their titles or "the honorable." Too few of us are doing this today, and it's very bad manners.

- **Be sensitive to the culture, religious laws and diet of international friends and colleagues.** Brief yourself on their country before you see them. Know their country's leading politicians, the names of their country's great museums, their universities and what types of foods they can and cannot eat.

- **Watch your table manners.** This can never be stressed enough. Don't stuff food in your mouth or talk while eating. Do not leave your dirty napkin on the table, when you excuse yourself during a meal. Leave it on your chair instead. Wipe your mouth frequently. When finished, move your fork and knife to the right-hand rim of the plate—and sit up straight. Ignoring these things makes you appear rather uncouth.

- **Don't monopolize the guest of honor.** Give equal time to every guest, regardless of how important or unimportant his/her position. This is an act of kindness as well as good manners.

- **Teach your students to respect their elders.** Have them stand up when your friends enter the room...say,"How do you do?"...and shake hands. Parents seem to be failing in this, perhaps because they are not around their children as much these days. But making the effort will make your children's lives much easier as adults.

- **Know how and when to apologize.** Always make your apology as soon as possible after the event. Some acts require only a spoken apology, others require a spoken and written apology...and some require much more.

- **<u>Write thank you notes for gifts, favors, meals or any act of kindness</u>**. Also write notes to encourage congratulate and commiserate.

CAMPUS MINISTRIES INFO

Campus Ministries

The teenage population will grow from 19 million to 33 million from 1994 to 2004. 88% of teens don't attend church anywhere on a regular basis. If nothing changes, some estimate that only 4% of American teens will be attending church by the year 2004. Over 80% of people who trust Christ as savior do so by the time they turn 18. It is extremely urgent the church aggressively and strategically reaches out to the American teenager.[4]

Equal Access Act

In 1984, the United States Congress passed the Equal Access Act, which guaranteed the students' Constitutional right to have "Religious" or Christian clubs on their public secondary school campuses. President Ronald Reagan then signed it into law.

In June of 1990, the United States Supreme Court upheld the Equal Access Act in a landmark decision handed down in Board of Education of Westside Community Schools vs. Mergens, (496 U.S. 226). This provided a vehicle for students to come together and meet at school, using the school facilities just like everyone else.

According to the American Center for Law and Justice, "the Supreme Court ruled that public secondary schools which receive federal funds and allow non-curriculum related clubs to meet on campus must also allow 'religious clubs' (that is, Bible clubs, Prayer clubs, or any club involving religious speech) to meet on campus during non-instructional time. . . . In other words, the school must give the religious club official recognition on campus. If the school allows service clubs, such as Interact, Zonta, or 4-H, or clubs like a chess club, it must allow religious clubs. This is what is meant by "equal access."

What about "separation of church and state?" Nowhere does the Constitution of the United States use the phrase "separation of church and state"! Neither is it in the Bill of Rights. The first time that the phrase is used is in a letter to the Danbury Baptist

---

[4] http://www.fpoa.org/content.asp?id=123

Association by Thomas Jefferson 14 years after the adoption of the Bill of Rights. The only governmental document to provide such a guarantee is the constitution of the former Union of Soviet Socialist Republics (USSR). What the First Amendment to the Constitution does say about religion is this: "Congress shall make no law respecting an establishment of religion or prohibiting the free exercise thereof . . ." In other words, the Federal Government is forbidden, by the First Amendment, from establishing or creating an official national religion. The government is also forbidden from passing any law which restricts, in any way, your right to practice your religion anytime, anyplace and anyway that you see fit.

First Priority

Mission Statement: First Priority exists for the purpose of reaching and discipling the next generation for Jesus Christ.

First Priority is a City-Wide vision

Shared by Local Churches

To Build a Comprehensive Strategy

And Provide Relevant Resources

That will Encourage, Equip, and Empower

Students, Parents, Leaders, and Churches

To Unite in Your Community and on Campus

To Reach, To Care for and To Disciple

A Generation for JESUS CHRIST

How First Priority Works

First Priority Builds A Network of Churches in your community

Committed to equipping students to reach their generation

By training and providing them the resources they need.

UNITY

First Priority Builds A Network of Students on each campus

Committed to reaching their school for Christ

By living like Christ and carrying out a plan to share their faith.

STRATEGY

First Priority Builds A Network of Parents/Adults around each school

Committed to model for students how to live and share their faith

By praying together and volunteering their time.

MENTORING

First Priority builds A Network of Business/Community Leaders in your city

Committed to helping students change their world

By financially supporting them and becoming personally involved.

SUPPORT

Youth for Christ

Since 1944, Youth for Christ has had a distinctive history of youth evangelism. In the early 1940s, during World War II, many young men, mostly ministers and evangelists, were holding large rallies in Canada, England and the United States. As the hunger for God's Word grew it became evident that there needed to be someone to coordinate this movement, providing leadership, strategy, and coordinating speakers, musicians and locations. Beginning in dozens of cities at the end of World War II, YFC quickly organized into a national movement. Billy Graham became YFC's first full-time staff member.

Starting with Saturday night youth rallies in the late 1940s and early 1950s, YFC's ministry methodology turned to Bible Clubs in the late 50s and 60s. It was in this period of ministry that the concept of teen to teen evangelism was birthed. Then in the middle sixties and early seventies Campus Life and Campus Life Middle School ministries to senior and junior high youth began to be the thrust of YFC ministry. Since that time there have been several ministry models that have been created. Youth Guidance became an avenue in reaching at-risk and institutionalized young people. Teen Parents developed to mentor and equip young parents with parenting skills as well as the love of Jesus Christ. City Life reaches the millions of young people in our neighborhoods and communities, partnering with the church and other organizations. Ministries are tailored to reach youth in urban, suburban, and rural settings.

In addition, YFC sponsors the DC/LA Student Evangelism SuperConferences, held every three years, designed to challenge and equip thousands of young people from hundreds of youth groups to effectively impact their schools for Christ.

YFC/USA is a chartered program of Youth for Christ International. Over 1,861 paid staff members and 16,571 volunteers serve in over 100 countries around the world. As a part of the YFC/USA commitment to serve the world, we offer Project Serve which provides overseas short-term mission opportunities. In addition, well over 100 YFC staff members from the U.S. have ministry assignments with YFC programs in other nations as part of YFC/USA's World Outreach Division.

Throughout YFC's history there has been an unwavering commitment to youth evangelism and biblical Christianity. One of YFC's slogans over the past fifty years has been "Anchored to the Rock, Geared to the Times"-the message of the gospel will never change and YFC is flexible to creatively communicate this message of hope, grace and love in the context of different cultural settings.

The YFC Campus Life ministry combines healthy relationships with creative programs to help senior high young people make good choices, establish a solid foundation for life, and positively impact their schools. Like every ministry of YFC, Campus Life seeks to engage these young people wherever they are found as life-long followers of Jesus Christ. Campus Life is a place for high school students to have fun, make friends and talk about matters to other high school students. Campus Life provides a balanced approach - physical, mental, social and spiritual - to give teens the skills and hope they need to live in a turbulent world. Campus Life club generally meets in various homes each week, hosted by students. In some cities, Campus Life may own a building they use to host club meetings, or have access to a school gym, cafeteria or classroom, or, less frequently, churches.

Campus Life MS offers junior high and middle school students opportunities for friendship, fun, and growth. Club meetings can be a great time to meet and "hang out" with kids from school, and a chance to talk about what's important to them. Besides weekly, topical meetings, there are area events, trips and special outings designed for the needs of young teens and the chance to get to know kids from other area schools. Staff and adult volunteers find creative ways to build relationships and communicate the life-changing message of Jesus Christ. Staff and volunteers provide leadership that kids can rely upon, as well as, providing a positive role model.

Young Life

Young Life, which began in 1941, is a non-profit organization committed to making an impact on kids' lives and preparing them for the future. Young Life leaders leave the comfort of their adult worlds and enter the arena of high school and middle school life. You will find Young Life leaders sitting in the stands at football games, walking the streets of inner-city neighborhoods, driving carloads of kids to the shopping malls or tutoring students in study centers after school. In fact, you will find them almost anywhere you can find kids. Young Life leaders model trust, respect and responsibility to their young friends, and they do it within a meaningful context, within the context of a teenager's world.

Young Life provides healthy, creative fun and aims to keep kids safe. From weekly clubs to seasonal camping experiences to daily outings with leaders, Young Life is known around the world as the organization that knows how to have fun.

Club typically meets once a week and has been described as an experience in "controlled chaos." Leaders combine songs, humor and group interaction to create an hour of energetic fun where kids can express that teenage tendency to push the limits -- but within the controlled context of a safe environment.

"Young Life" is the name of our organization, and it's also what we call our outreach to high school-aged kids. We have named our middle school ministry "WyldLife" to differentiate between the two age groups and their varying developmental stages and maturity levels. Both ministries stay true to the time-tested practices we've been using for more than 60 years: going where kids are, loving them unconditionally, earning the right to be heard and communicating God's love in terms kids can understand.

Young Life is active in all 50 states and more than 45 countries, reaching an estimated 1 million teenagers annually. More than 90,000 kids spend a weekend during the school year or a week during the summer at one of Young Life's 24 camping properties in the United States and Canada.

Our Vision

Every adolescent will have the opportunity to meet Jesus Christ and follow Him.

Our Mission

Introducing adolescents to Jesus Christ and helping them grow in their faith. We accomplish our mission by ...

Praying for young people.

Going where kids are.

Building personal relationships with them.

Winning the right to be heard.

Providing experiences that are fun, adventurous and life-changing.

Sharing our lives and the Good News of Jesus Christ with adolescents.

Inviting them to personally respond to this Good News.

Loving them regardless of their response.

Nurturing kids so they might grow in their love for Christ and the knowledge of God's Word and become people who can share their faith with others.

Helping young people develop the skills, assets and attitudes to reach their full God-given potential.

Encouraging kids to live connected to the Body of Christ by being an active member of a local congregation.

Working with a team of like-minded individuals -- volunteer leaders, committee members, donors and staff.

Our Values

Living according to and communicating the whole Gospel of Jesus Christ.

Carrying out our mission under the authority of Scripture and relying on the Holy Spirit to empower our ministry.

Encouraging the welfare and spiritual health of those who do this ministry, that they may minister out of a consistent and growing relationship with Christ and His followers.

Researching and developing innovative approaches to reaching uncommitted, disinterested kids around the world.

Reaching adolescents of all social, cultural, economic and ethnic backgrounds throughout the world.

Working with followers of Christ from a variety of traditions and local churches around the world.

Welcoming all those whom God calls to our mission -- men and women of all races, staff and volunteers -- who are linked to a common purpose of introducing adolescents to Jesus Christ.

Observing the highest standards of stewardship of all the resources placed in our trust.

Student Venture

Student Venture is the high school and junior high ministry of <u>Campus Crusade for Christ International</u>. Since 1966, Student Venture has been reaching out to teenagers with more than 1300 full-time staff, Student Venture affiliates, and local community volunteers. Student Venture is a contributing member of the Campus Alliance and National Network of Youth Ministries©. Through the Campus Alliance, Student Venture and 60 other national organizations are working hand in hand to help develop campus movements so that every student at every campus has the opportunity to grow in character and know Christ.

Where Is Student Venture?

Student Venture is currently serving in <u>20 metro locations</u> and over <u>100 affiliate locations</u> in the U.S. <u>Contact us</u> nationally.

Our Purpose

The mission of Student Venture is to give every teenager the opportunity to hear the truth and love of Jesus Christ, to grow in their faith relationship with Him, and to reach others with the message of Christ. We call it Win – Build – Send.

Our Plan

Reach the Campus, Reach the World - By focusing on the campus, we make contact with the greatest number of teenagers in a community. In Student Venture, our strategy is comprehensive:

Student Venture Field Teams – Working in communities to win, build and send students at local campuses.

The Coaching Center – Coaching adults and students by phone and Internet to reach teenagers and schools.

Student Venture Media Resources – Using Internet, video, radio, television and print media to reach teenagers.

Student Venture International Partnerships – Teaming internationally to reach teenagers.

Our People

Student Venture's ministry extends to thousands of students led by more than 600 full-time staff, interns, Student Venture affiliates and local community volunteers. Our heart and passion is loving Christ and loving teenagers.

Why Reach the Campus?

by Chuck Klein - National Director, Student Venture

For more than thirty years I have been reaching students on high school campuses. It is pure pleasure spending time with teenagers, relating to them in their fast-paced, ever-changing world.

The high school and junior high campuses of our nation and the world are what I call the marketplace of youth culture. For teenagers, it is where the exchange of ideas, the forming of values, and the shaping of lives take place. Once a student hits junior and senior high school, the influence of the home often diminishes, replaced by the powerful influence of peers. The teen culture is reshaping students so dramatically that parents often find they now have a stranger in their home. For a rapidly growing number of teenagers worldwide, this on-campus culture is where life makes up its mind. Lives are being shaped every day at our neighborhood schools.

But more than a cultural center, junior and senior high schools serve as magnets in a community, gathering people together as no other institution in our society. Think about it. Where are most teenagers on any given Monday through Friday, August to June? The answer: the local school. And it is the last time this entire age group is going to be together in one location. After high school they scatter throughout society, making it much more difficult to reach them personally. As 13-to-18-year-olds, they are at an age of responsiveness to the gospel, and they are gaining maturity to make life-long commitments to Jesus Christ. Think of the number of teenagers who would be reached if there were a relevant witness for Christ at every school worldwide. Think of the impact as these teens enter into society, already committed to Jesus Christ. And think of the parents who would be touched as well, for one cannot reach kids without influencing the family.

Reach the campus, and you will reach the world. There is not a more strategic ministry in all of society. It is a ministry that takes a sizable commitment: on-site workers who love teenagers and have a passion to communicate truth; technology to reach teenagers using every form of media; and above all, an army of investors who pray and partner with local and national ministries to accomplish the task.

Kids are like wet cement, just waiting for someone to leave a lasting impression. We have the opportunity to leave that lasting impression for Christ.

Fellowship of Christian Athletes (FCA)

The Fellowship of Christian Athletes is touching millions of lives... one heart at a time. Since 1954, the Fellowship of Christian Athletes has been challenging coaches and athletes on the professional, college, high school, junior high and youth levels to use the powerful medium of athletics to impact the world for Jesus Christ. FCA is the largest interdenominational, school-based, Christian sports organization in America. FCA focuses on serving local communities by equipping, empowering and encouraging people to make a difference for Christ.

The FCA Vision

To see the world impacted for Jesus Christ through the influence of athletes and coaches.

The FCA Mission

To present to athletes and coaches and all whom they influence the challenge and adventure of receiving Jesus Christ as Savior and Lord, serving Him in their relationships and in the fellowship of the church.

The FCA Values

Our relationships will demonstrate steadfast commitment to Jesus Christ and His Word through Integrity, Serving, Teamwork and Excellence.

FCA's Heritage

1954   FCA incorporated by its founder, Don McClanen. Paul Benedum, Branch Rickey and other Pittsburgh businessmen underwrote the first year's budget. Charter members included Otto Graham, Carl Erskine, Donn Moomaw and Rickey.

1956   First National Camp at Estes Park, Colorado with 256 athletes and coaches attending. FCA moves its national headquarters from Norman, Oklahoma to Kansas City, Missouri.

1959   The Christian Athlete magazine was first published.

1960   Lake Geneva, Wisconsin, joins Estes Park as the second FCA Camp site.

1964   Adult Chapter program begun. First National Camp at Black Mountain, North Carolina.

1966   Huddle program established.

1967   FCA holds eight National Camps with 4,700 participants.

1968   National Coaches Conferences initiated.

1969   FCA holds a record 16 National Camps with more than 7,000 attendees. FCA huddles exceed 1,000.

1972   Huddles exceed 1,500. Adult Chapters grow to 200. Full time-staffers increase to 23.

1974   National Conference Center (NCC) opened near Marshall, Indiana. Women's Ministry established.

1977   National Golf Ministry launched. Huddles increase to 2,000.

1978   FCA staff grows to more than 100. FCA holds 32 National Camps.

1979   National Headquarters Building and Chapel dedicated.

1982   Sharing the VICTORY magazine published, replacing The Christian Athlete.

1985   4,400 official Huddles and 220 FCA employees in 34 states.

1987   National Summer Camps held at 34 sites; 4,300 coaches and spouses at 17 National Coaches meetings.

1989   Four-court indoor gym dedicated at NCC. CHAD principle introduced. Some 40,000 athletes/coaches/adults official FCA members; 275 FCA staff in 42 states; 100,000 student athletes meeting in Huddles during school year.

1991 FCA produces a booklet dealing with drug abuse and introduces the "One Way 2 Play Drug Free" program and charter.

1993 Camp attendance exceeds 10,000. Huddles top 5,000 for the first time in history.

1994 320 staff members, an all time high nationally. FCA's 40th Anniversary.

1995 13,048 attend FCA National Camps. We become established on the World Wide Web at www.fca.org.

1996 One Way to Play-Drug FREE! video is released. FCA celebrates 40 years of Camps at Estes Park, Colorado.

1997 FCA presents its mission internationally with the 'Global Initiative'. Huddles grow to 6,598.

1998 The Home Office announces the plan to more than double the size of the existing building. Over 10,000 golfers take part in the FCA National Golf Scramble.

1999 FCA receives 100,000 One Way 2 Play! commitments.

2000 Vice Presidential candidate Dick Cheney comes to FCA World Headquarters to endorse FCA and One Way 2 Play! program.
-Groundbreaking on World Headquarters building expansion.

2002 Dedication of 59,000-square foot World Headquarters.
-FCA introduces "4 C's" concept (Coaches, Campus, Camps, Community)

2003 FCA Baseball Ministry launched
-FCA launches Team FCA membership program.

2004 FCA celebrates 50 years of ministry.

Youth Alive (Assemblies of God)

Why & How to Start a Club?

A campus club is a great place for students to engage the Bible and its teachings together. Such campus clubs are supported by the Equal Access Act and have been upheld by the United States Supreme Court. Do you know your rights as a student on your campus? We have a Student's Rights tool that summarizes your rights.

A campus club provides a place for Christians to gather and worship God. It also gives other students a place to come and discover God and His Word with you.

You are the perfect person to minister on your school campus. No teacher, pastor or parent can reach out to your friends as well as you. Youth Alive provides you materials to reach the lost and hurting on your campus. Does your school have an effective campus club for your to join? If so, get involved in it. If not, consider starting a Youth Alive campus club. Read on for more information.

A Youth Alive club is a student-initiated and led campus group that is…

TELLING . It presents the Message of hope to the campus through a variety of methods: See You At The Pole (SYATP), True Love Waits, The Bridge, Flip The Script, The Seven Project.

SERVICE-ORIENTED. It provides a service to the campus through various endeavors: clean-up days, canned food drives, holiday gifts and baskets for the less-fortunate, volunteer work for the school, its administration and faculty.

CHURCH-BASED. It seeks to maintain an open forum for all denominations and bridge a gap between students and the local church. It blends a multi-denominational effort to present the Gospel. It is a vehicle to enhance the entire Body of Christ on the campus. A Youth Alive club is a place where the Body of Christ joins together; not a place to define its differences through discussing divisive issues.

A SUPPORT COMMUNITY. It works to become a place where Christians on campus have the opportunity to: share needs with other students, request prayer, receive encouragement from God's Word.

6 Steps to Starting a Campus Club

STEP ONE: PRAY

Ask for God's wisdom and direction. "Do not be anxious about anything, but in everything, by prayer and petition, with thanksgiving, present your requests to God" (Philippians 4:6).

Pray for the approval process. "Then Jesus told his disciples a parable to show them that they should always pray and not give up…" (Luke 18:1).

Pray for God's favor upon your dream to start a club.

List adults in your church who will join you in prayer for this new campus club; Prayer Zone Partners [link to PZP 'What is it?'] helps enlist adults to join the continued prayer support for school communities.

STEP TWO: PREPARE

Make a list of students interested in forming a Youth Alive club. Use the Student Interest for Youth Alive Club [link].

Schedule an initial appointment with your principal: a) warmly approach him/her with the idea of starting a club (use Meeting With the Principal), b) inform him/her of your personal interest and share the list of students during your meeting, c) ask him/her to inform you of the school policy and procedure for pursuing the request, d) thank him/her for meeting with you, e) if you sense any apprehension from him/her, refer to Overcoming Obstacles, f) Step four will guide you through the formal request process. Use and complete the Youth Alive Preparation Sheet: a) refer to this sheet throughout the process of forming the club, b) portions of the information on this form will be valuable in your formal presentation.

STEP THREE: PEOPLE

Make a list of at least three businesses, churches and community leaders who will support the formation of your club: a) these community leaders will strengthen your effectiveness and provide a means of sponsorship for the club, b) many people are waiting for someone to ask them to make a difference on a local school campus, c) refer to can complete the Support Form, d) present this list to your principal or administration during your formal presentation.

If possible, identify a faculty advisor and list him/her on your Preparation Sheet.

STEP FOUR: PRESENT

Schedule a presentation appointment with the principal or administration of your school. Be organized. These items will help you make an excellent presentation: Build a Better Student, National Youth Alive Charter Application, Youth Alive Constitution, Preparation Sheet, Student Interest List, Business, Church and Community Support List, Faculty Advisor, Students' Rights and the Public Schools

Wear appropriate clothing.

Demonstrate a positive and respectful attitude. You may not receive an immediate answer to your request. Be patient, but be persistent.

If your presentation is initially denied, see Overcoming Obstacles and Students' Rights and the Public Schools.

STEP FIVE: PARTICIPATE

Upon approval, send in your completed National Youth Alive Charter Application.

Gain support. Youth Alive has a growing number of full-time district Youth Alive Directors ready to assist, train and help you as an official Youth Alive club. They can help you get the latest information on campus ministry events, and can assist you in finding legal helps. As a nationally-chartered club, you will receive four leadership newsletters full of inspiration and resources each school year. Once your application has been processed, you will receive a National Youth Alive Charter Certificate to be displayed in your school.

STEP SIX: TOOLS, TOOLS, TOOLS

Find all the resources you need for your campus ministry on this page. But first…

The Infield Strategy is the basis for how Youth Alive operates its's campus clubs. The method is simple: students empowered by the Holy Spirit and organized with a plan for their faith make an impact for God's Kingdom!

To use all of the concepts in the Infield Strategy, you need the something like the <u>Campus Ministry Playbook</u>. It provides an entire year of Infield Strategy programming and includes helps and ideas to keep your campus club strong and effective. Yet, you will find plenty of helps through this website to organize and operate your club.

Campus Missionary Packet

Step One: MAKE THE COMMITMENT

My Campus Missionary Commitment:

PRAY

I will pray each day that God will open the doors for campus ministry. (Colossians 4:2, 3; Thessalonians 3:1)

I will pray that Christians will take a stand and witness for Christ. (Matthew 9:38; Luke 10:2; Ephesians 6:19)

I will pray for the leaders—students, principals, teachers, and coaches. (1 Timothy 2:1, 2; Nehemiah 1:11)

I will pray for burnouts and hard-cases on campus (Psalm 2:8)

I will bind and cast down strongholds - humanism, "meism," materialism, secularism, false religions, dividing spirits. (Matthew 18:18—20; 2 Corinthians 10:3—6)

LIVE

I will live a life of daily devotion to Christ through the Word of God. (Matthew 4:4)

I will schedule a day of fasting and prayer each semester. (2 Chronicles 7:14)

I will love all Christians, regardless of denomination. (John 13:35)

I will be filled with the Spirit of God. (Ephesians 5:18)

TELL

I will identify, pray for, and maintain a list of at least three friends I will seek to daily witness the hope of Jesus Christ to. (Matthew 28:18-20)

I will use the classroom, extracurricular involvement, and other activities as a platform to share Christ. (1 Peter 3:15)

SERVE

I will encourage others to identify themselves as Christians on campus and establish a standard for how a Christian lives. (You're either a missionary or a mission field.) (Romans 1:16)

I will organize or participate regularly in an on-campus ministry that serves my campus. (Hebrews 10:24-25)

GIVE

As one missionary to another, I will give regularly and sacrificially to another mission work sponsored by my youth group or church.

I will exercise a giving heart toward all my service efforts on campus.